I kick for the KING OF KINGS!

**Written and Illustrated by
Antoinette Nnadi**

No part of this publication may be reproduced in whole or part, or stored in a retrieval system, or transmitted in any form or by any means, electronic, mechanical, photocopying, recording, or otherwise, without written permission of the publisher.

For information regarding permission, write to:
Children of Praise International Ministries
2807 Profitt Path
Edgewood, MD 21040

ISBN 978-1-7355899-5-4

Copyright @2021 by Antoinette Nnadi and Children of Praise Ministries.
All rights reserved.

DEDICATION

This book is dedicated to David and Diana Ibidapo and all of the children who love the Lord!

KEEP MOVING FOR HIM!

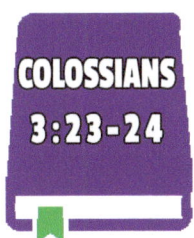

Love, Aunty Antoinette

WHEN I SAY MY ABCs

A B C

I applaud for the ALMIGHTY!

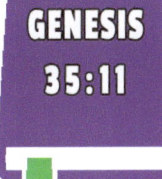
GENESIS 35:11

4

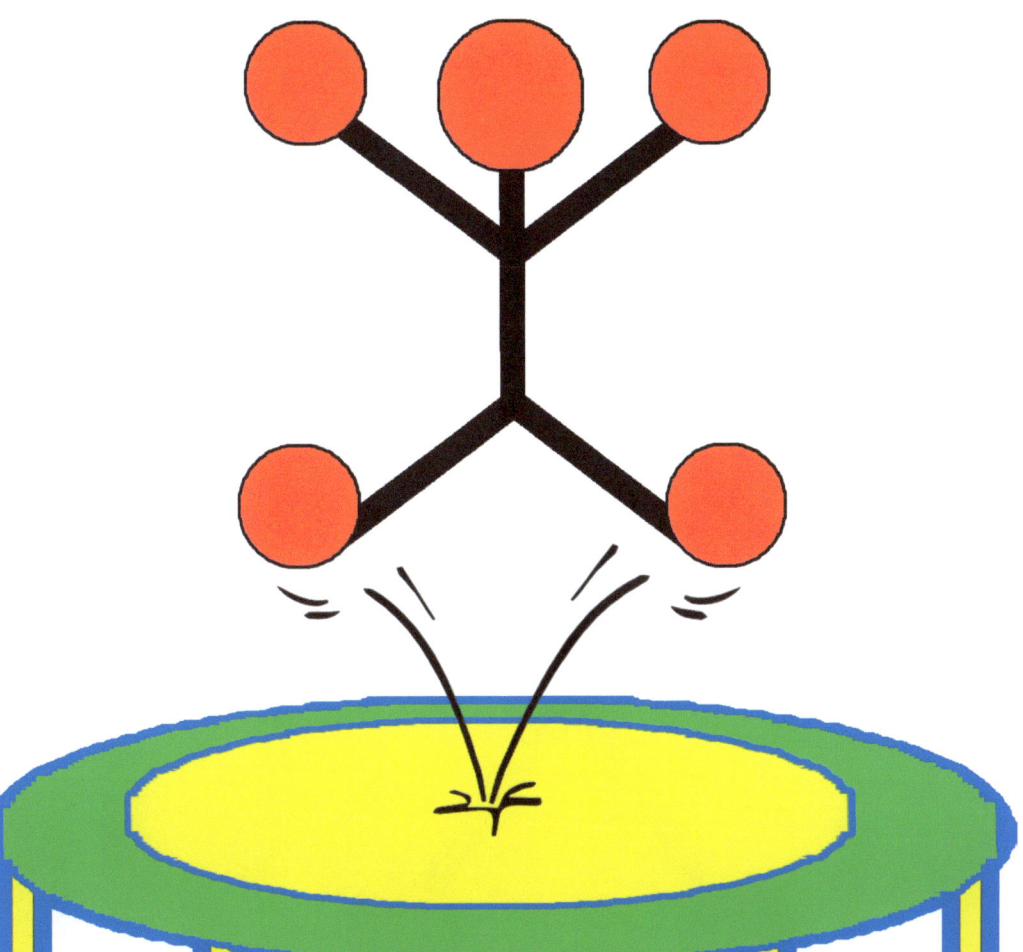

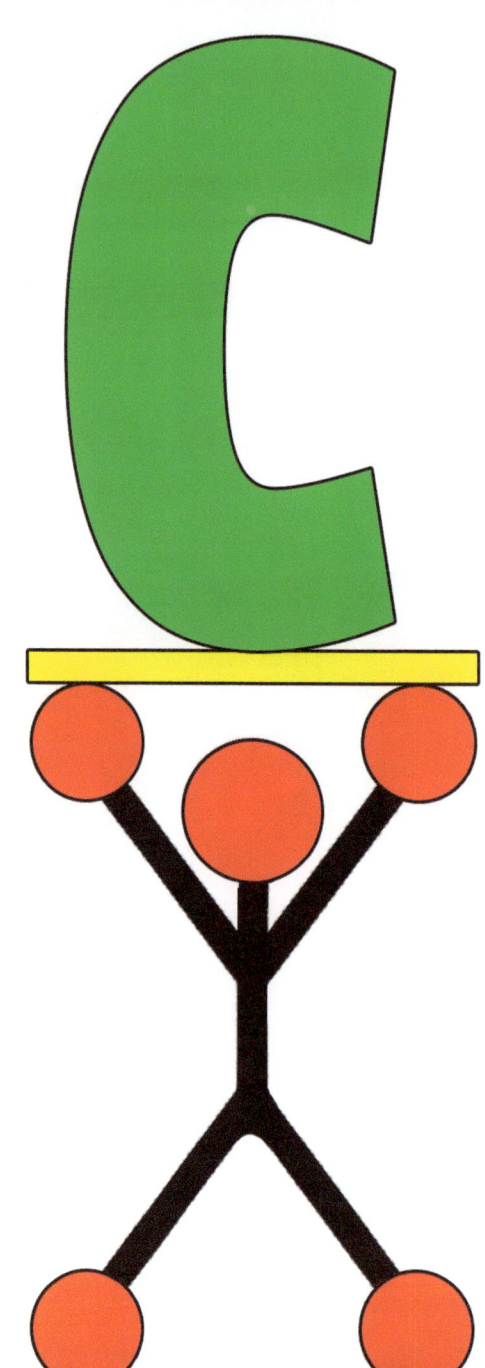

I climb for the CREATOR!

ISAIAH 40:28

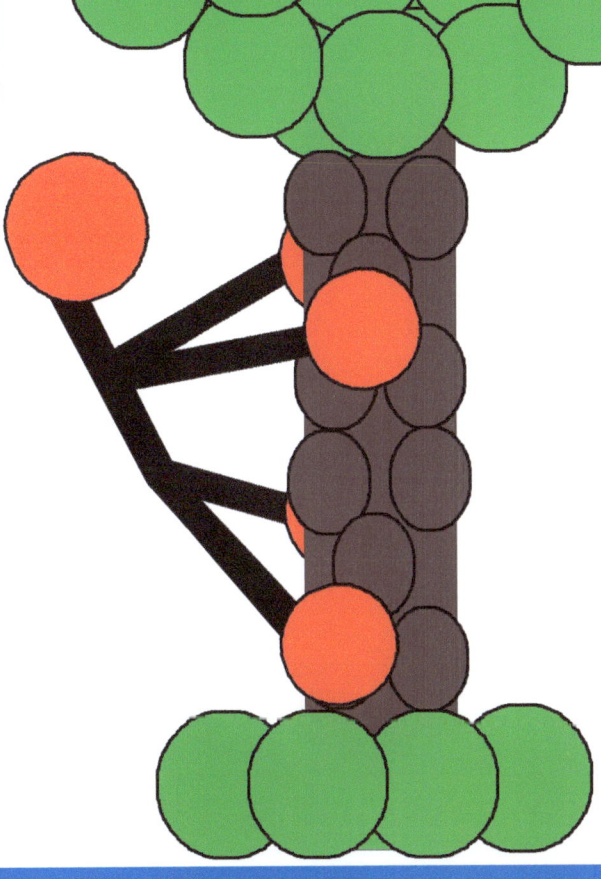

I dash for the DELIVERER!

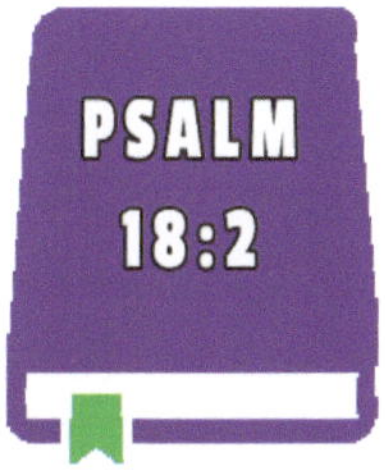

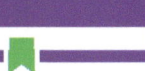

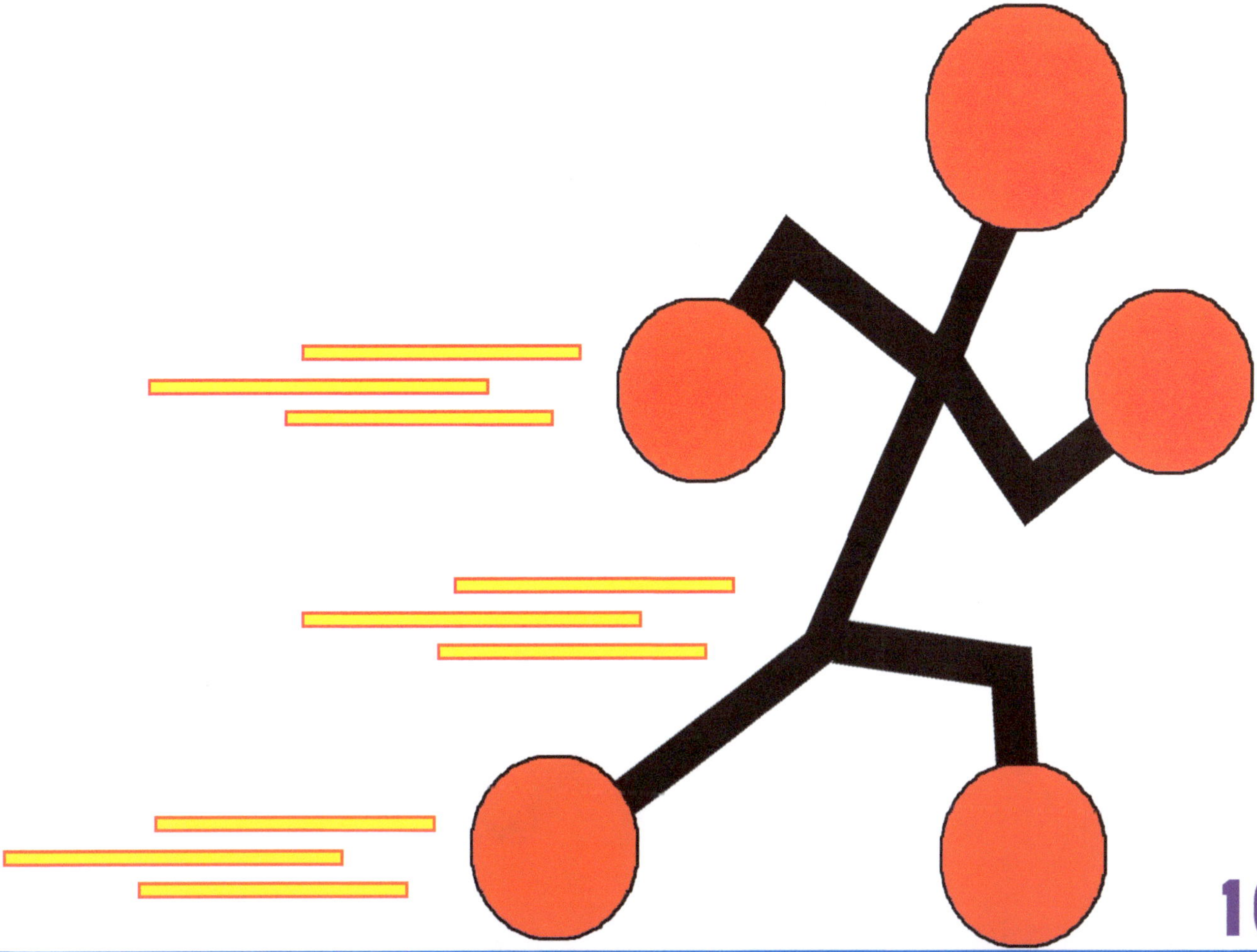

I exercise for ELOHIM!

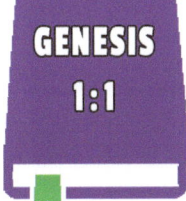

GENESIS 1:1

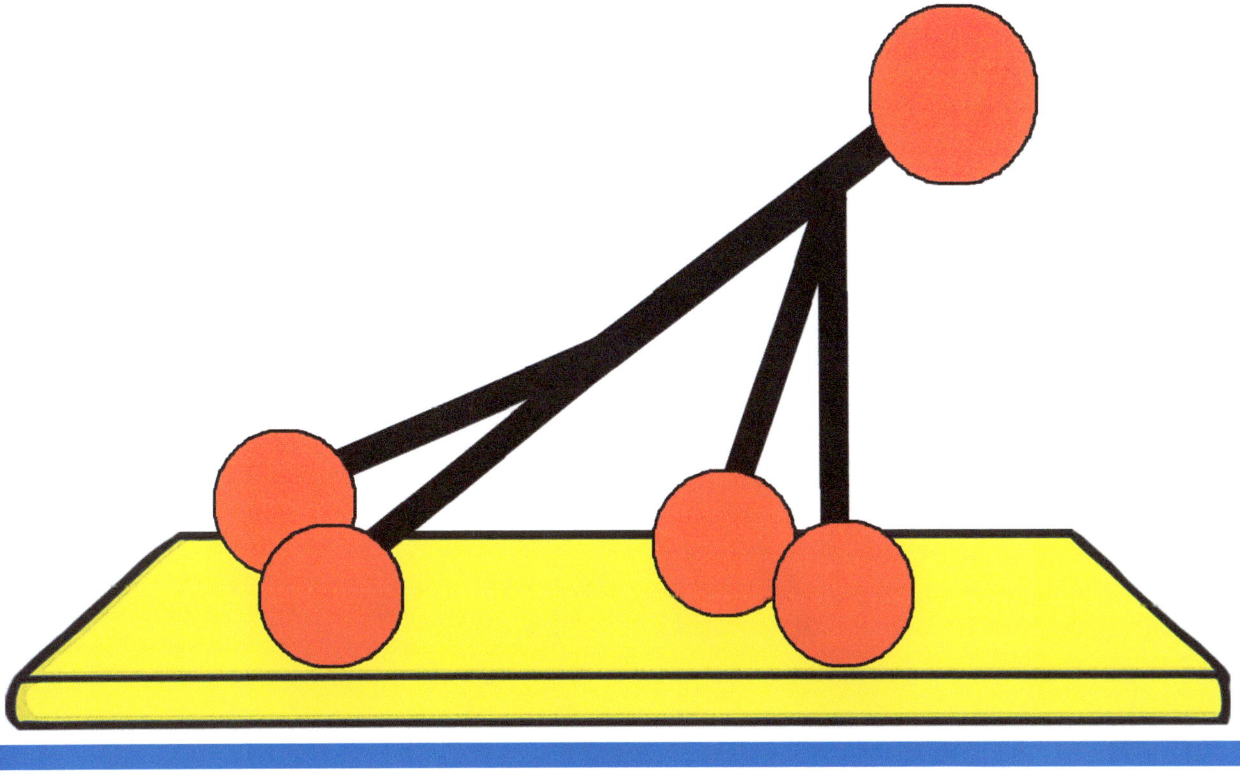

I fly for the FIRST AND THE LAST!

REVELATION 22:13

14

I glide for the GOOD SHEPHERD!

JOHN 10:11

16

I hop for the HOLY ONE!

ISAIAH 43:15

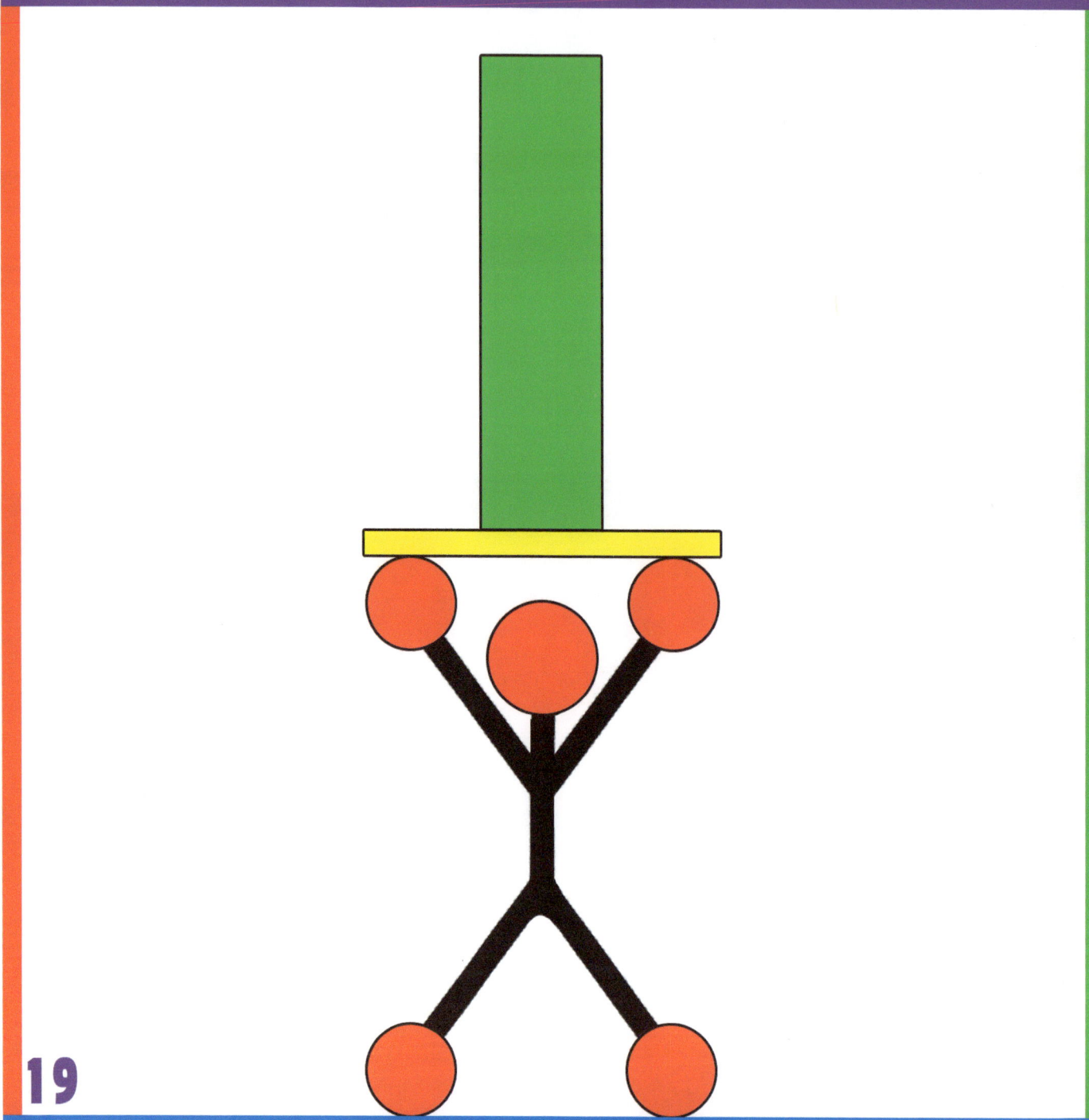

I invent for the I AM THAT I AM!

EXODUS 3:14

20

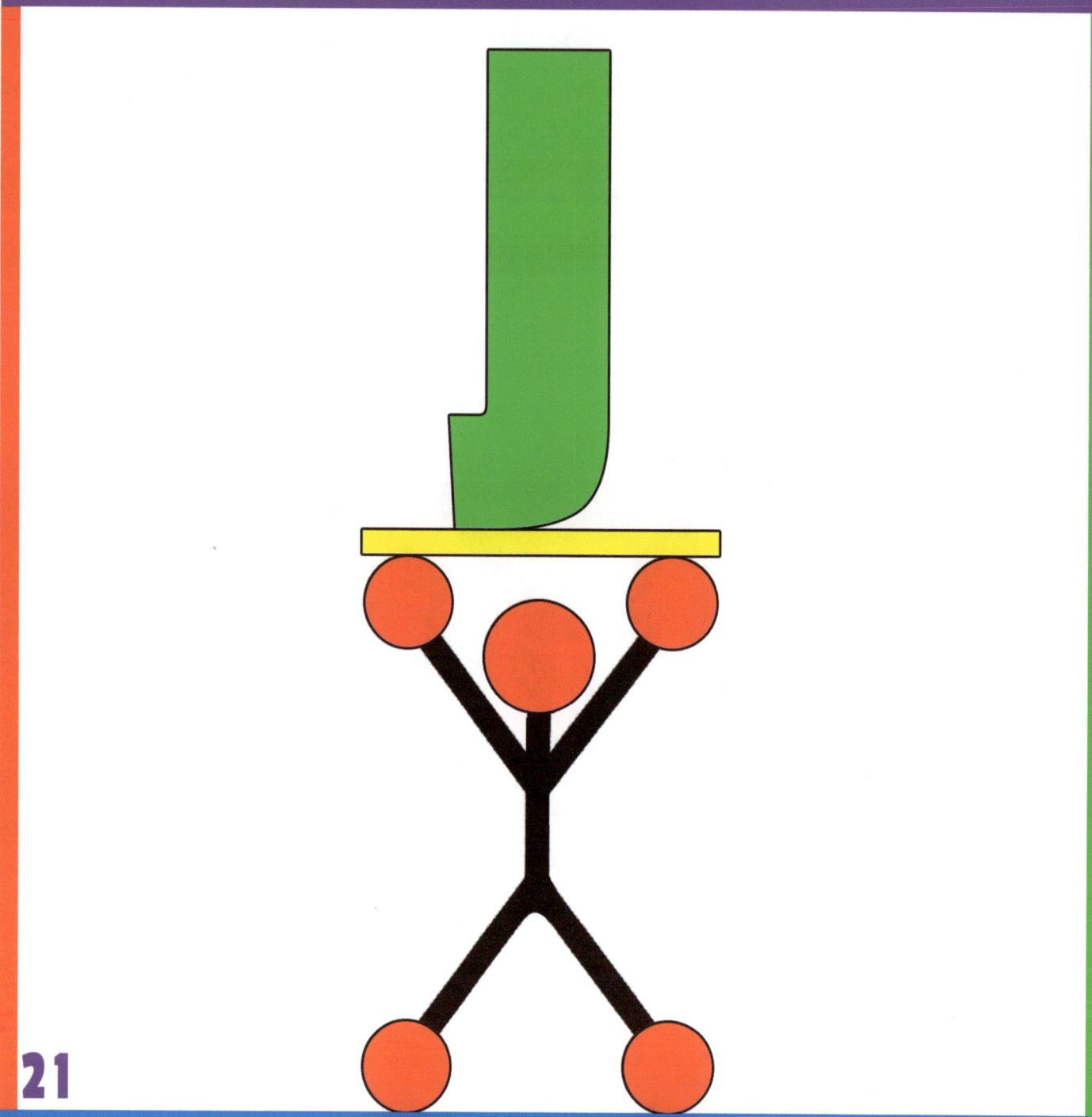

I jump for JEHOVAH!

PSALM 83:18

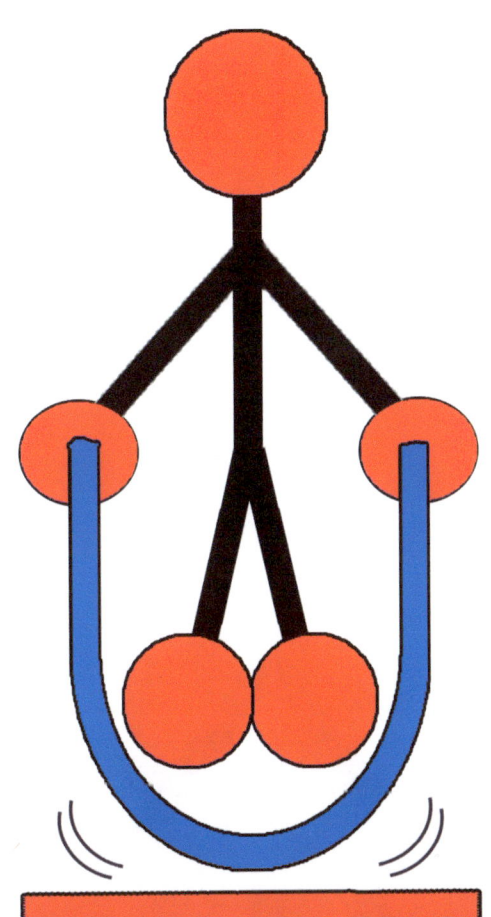

22

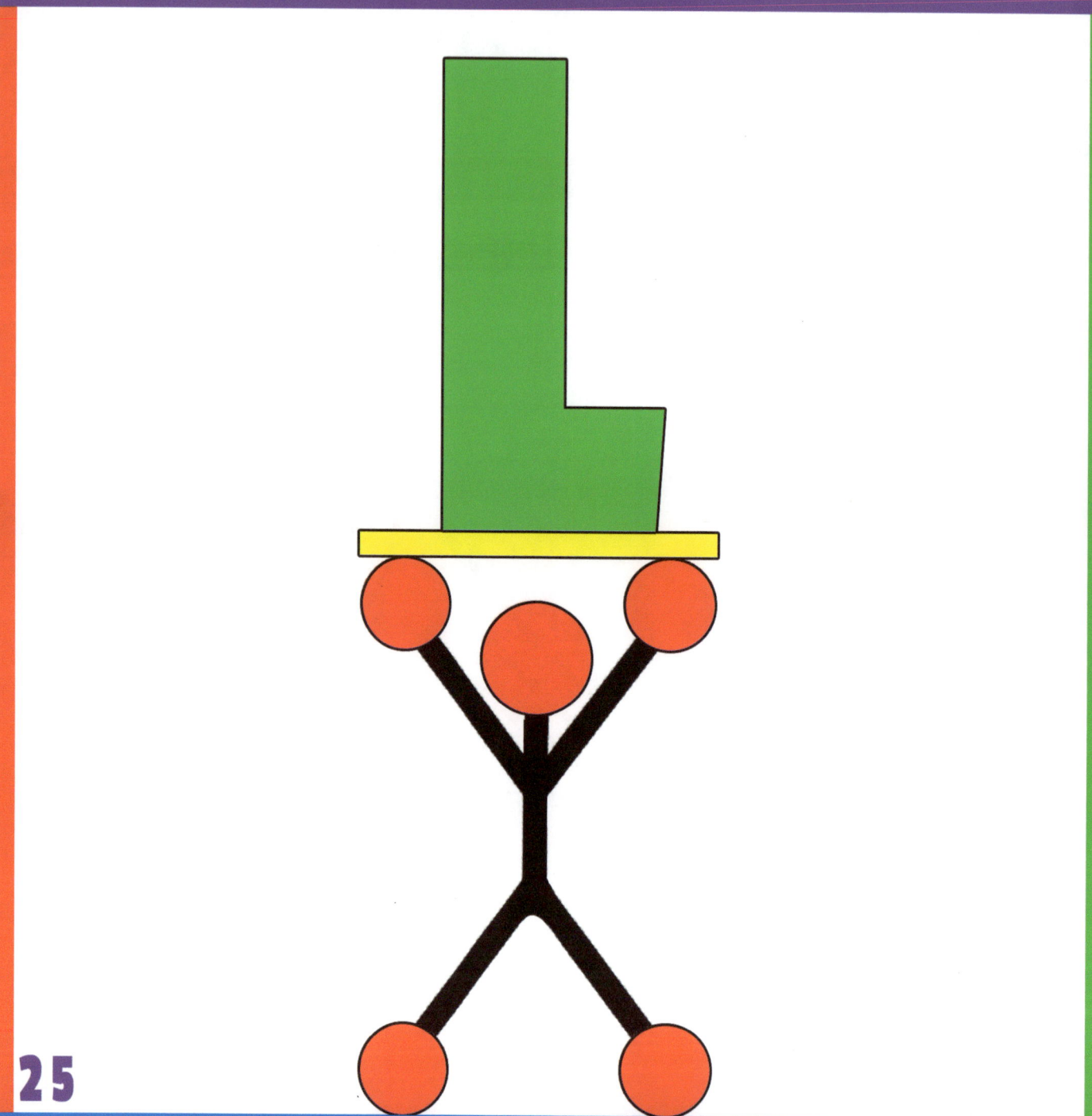

I leap for the LORD OF LORDS!

REVELATION 19:16

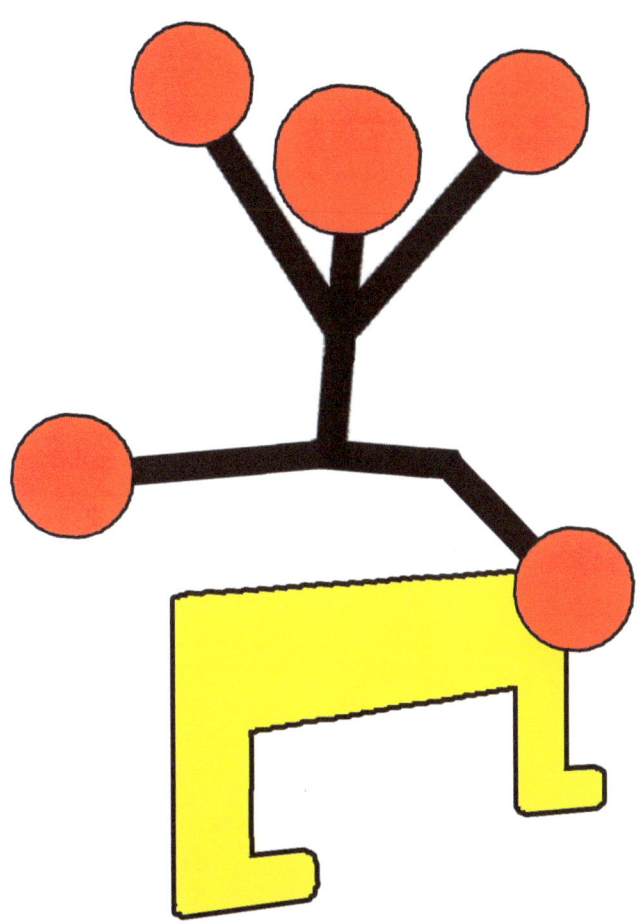

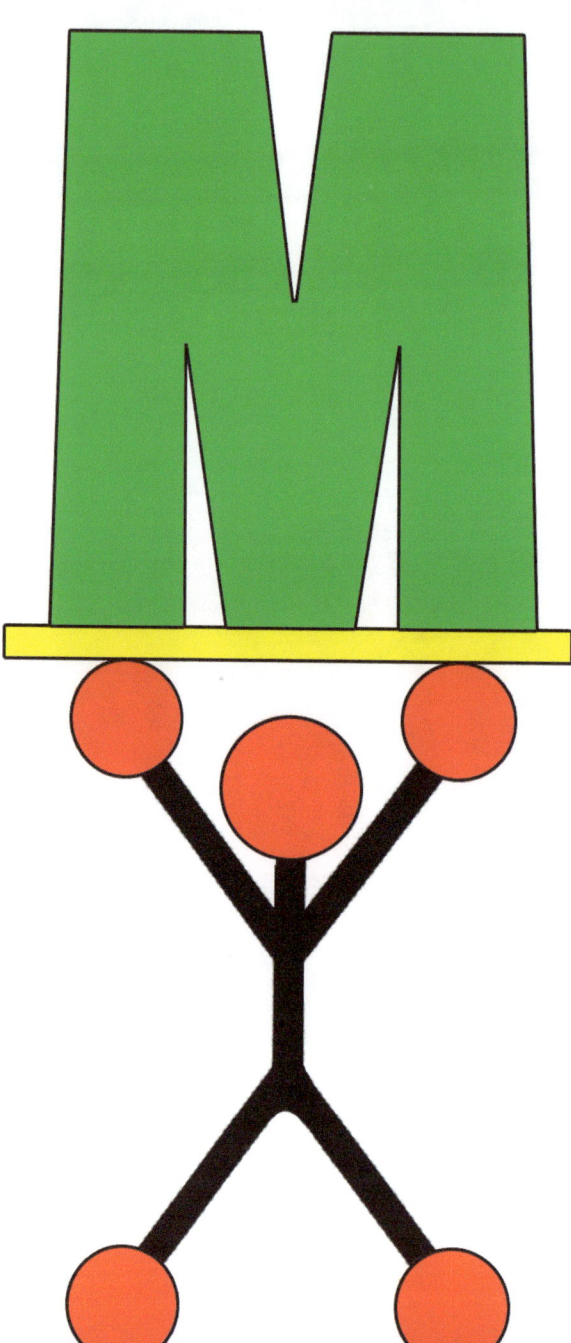

I march for the MESSIAH!

JOHN 4:25

I nap for the NAME ABOVE ALL NAMES!

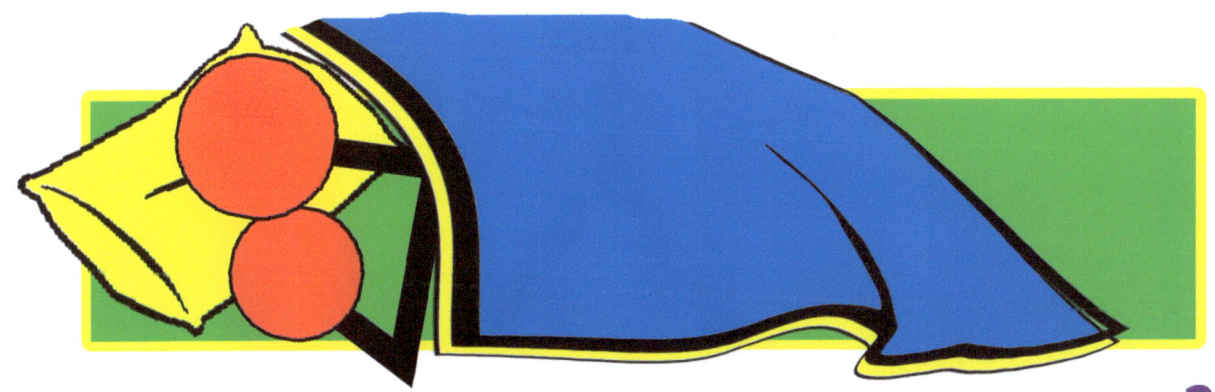

I organize for the OMNIPOTENT!

REVELATION 19:6

I paint for the PRINCE OF PEACE!

ISAIAH 9:6

I read for the REDEEMER!

JOB 19:25

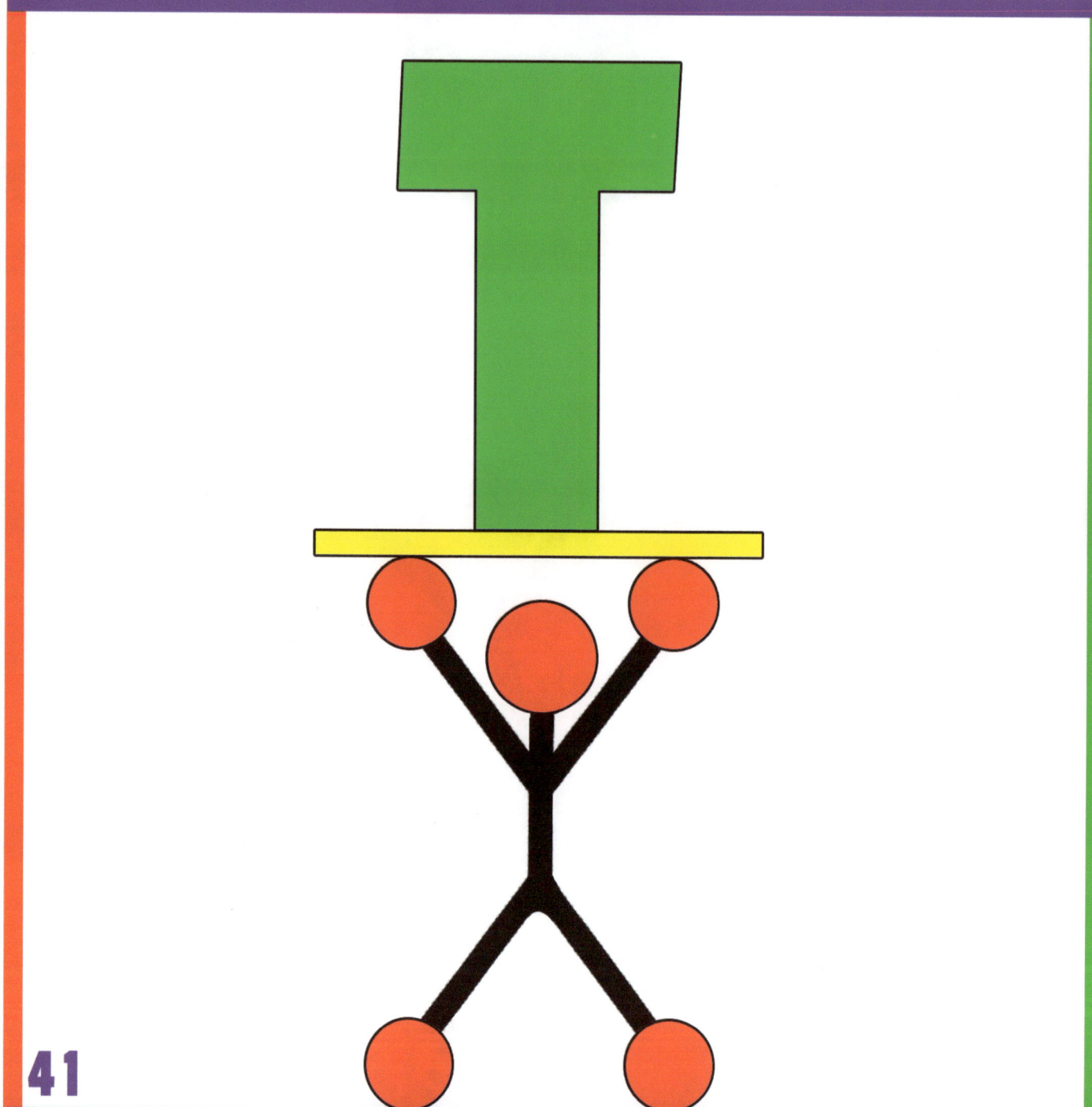

I throw for the TRUTH!

JOHN 14:6

42

43

I uplift for the UTMOST!

JEREMIAH 10:6

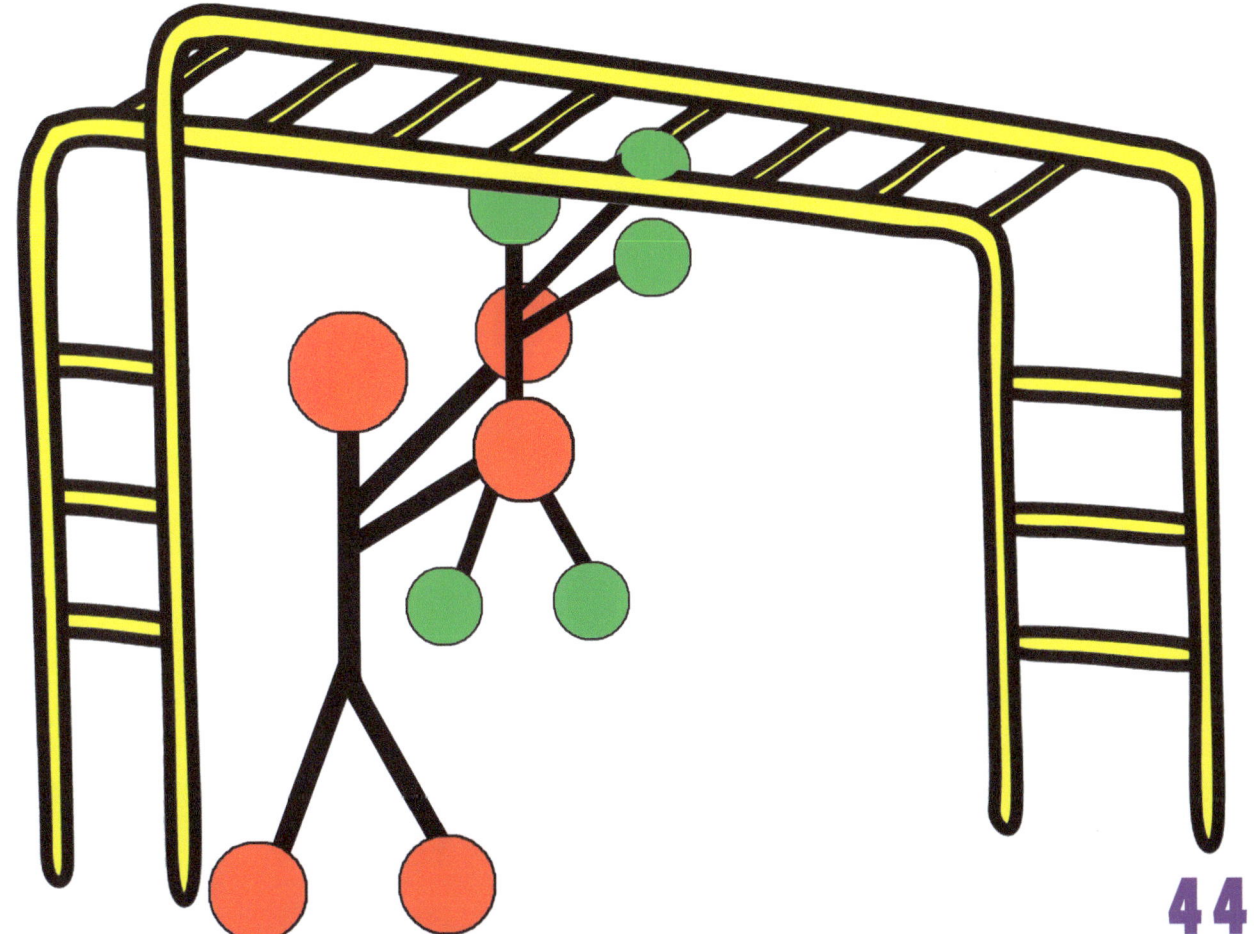

44

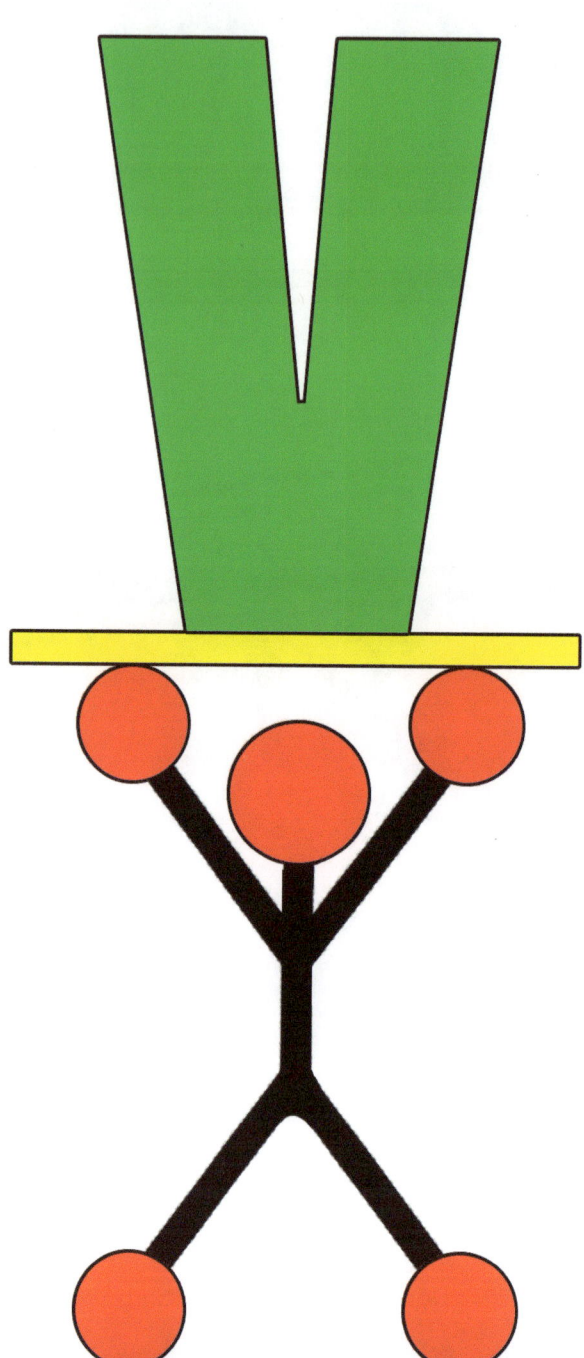

I vacuum for the TRUE VINE!

JOHN 15:1

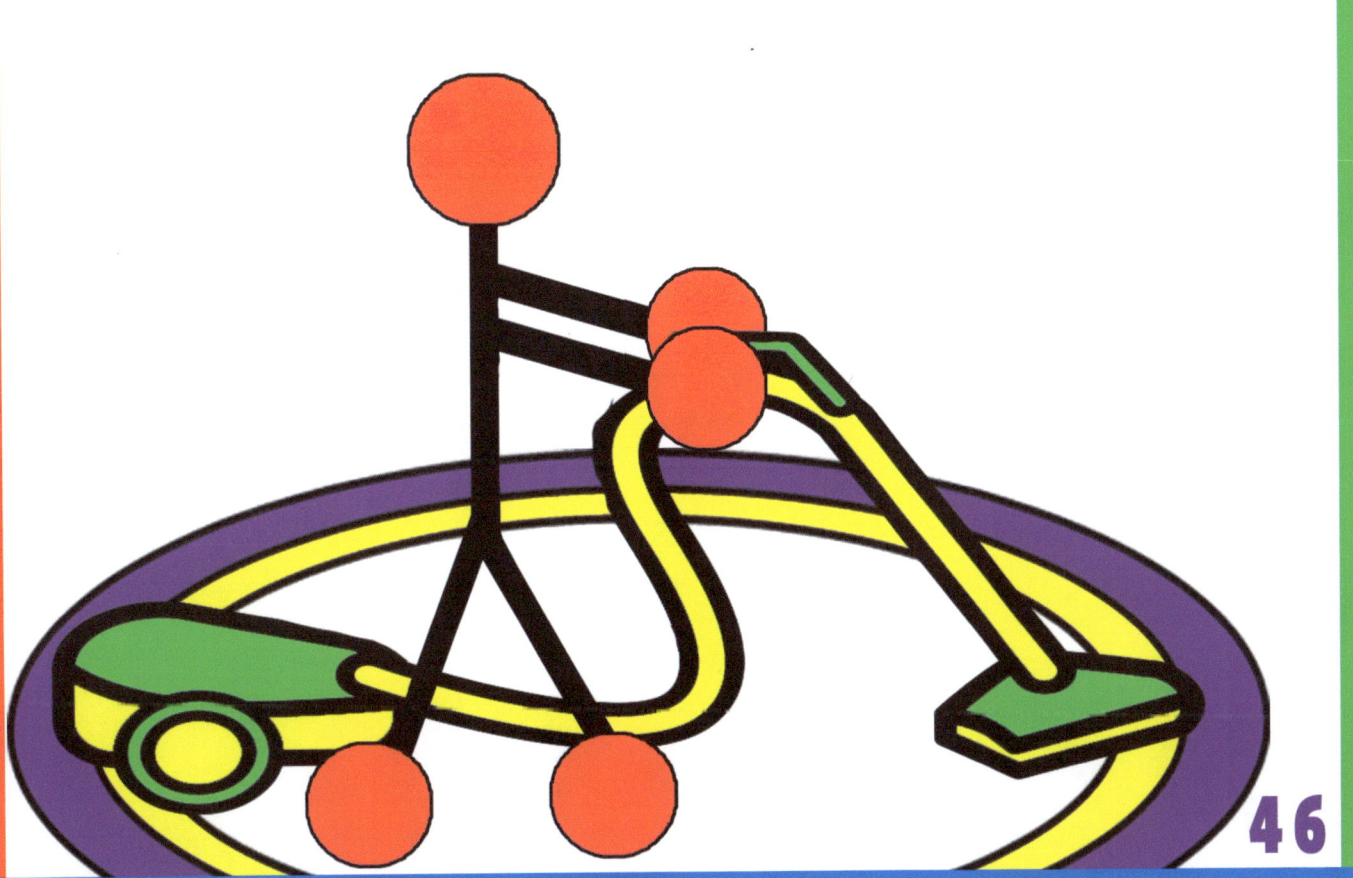

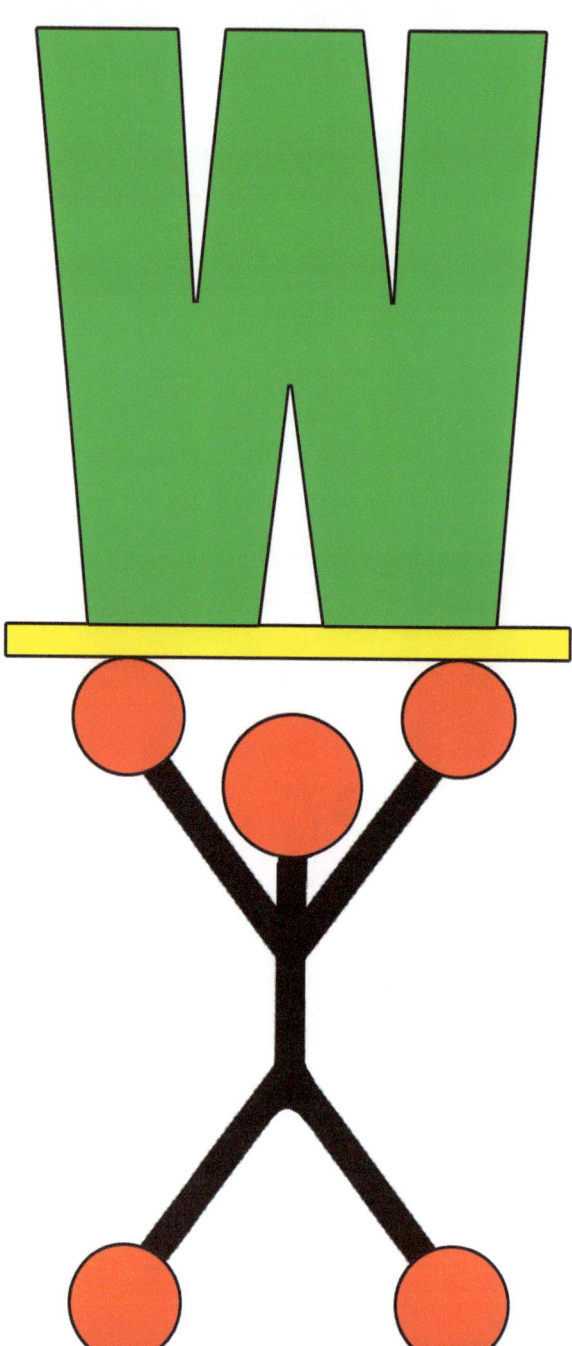

I whistle for the WORD!

JOHN 1:1

48

I am xenial for the eXtraordinary GOD!

I yank for YAHWEH!

LEVITICUS 18:2

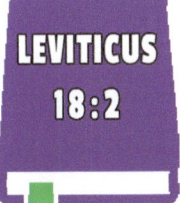

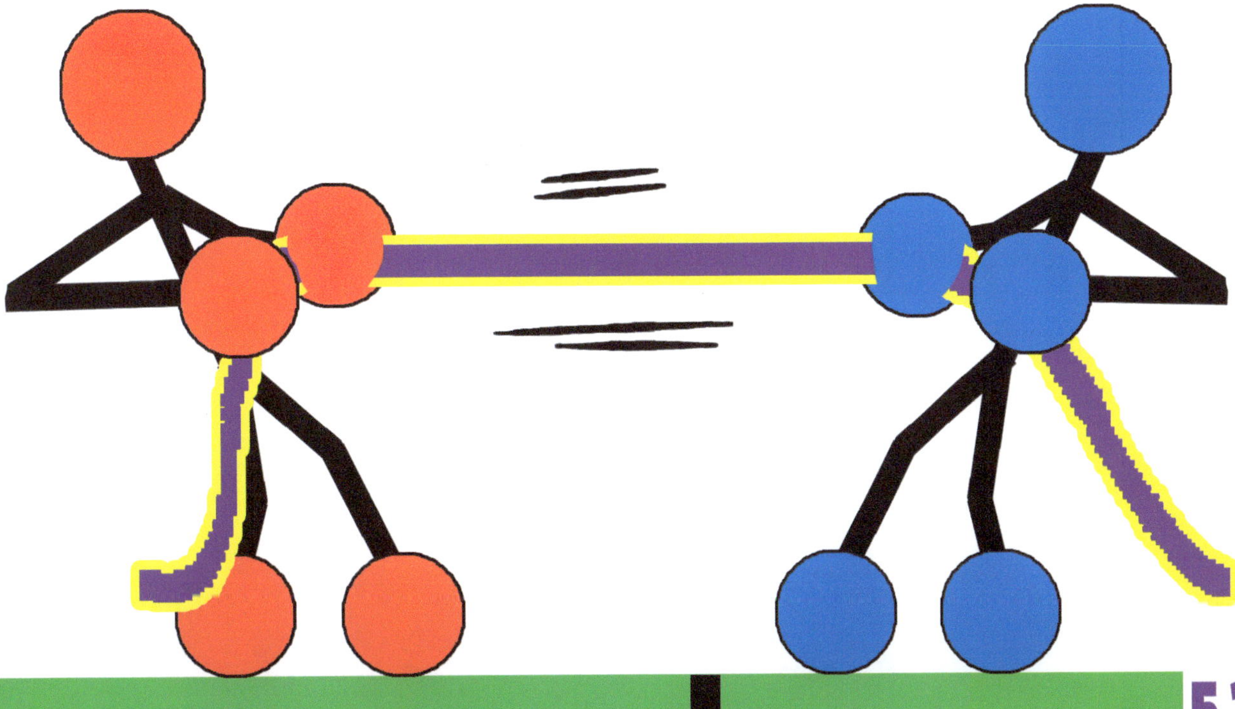

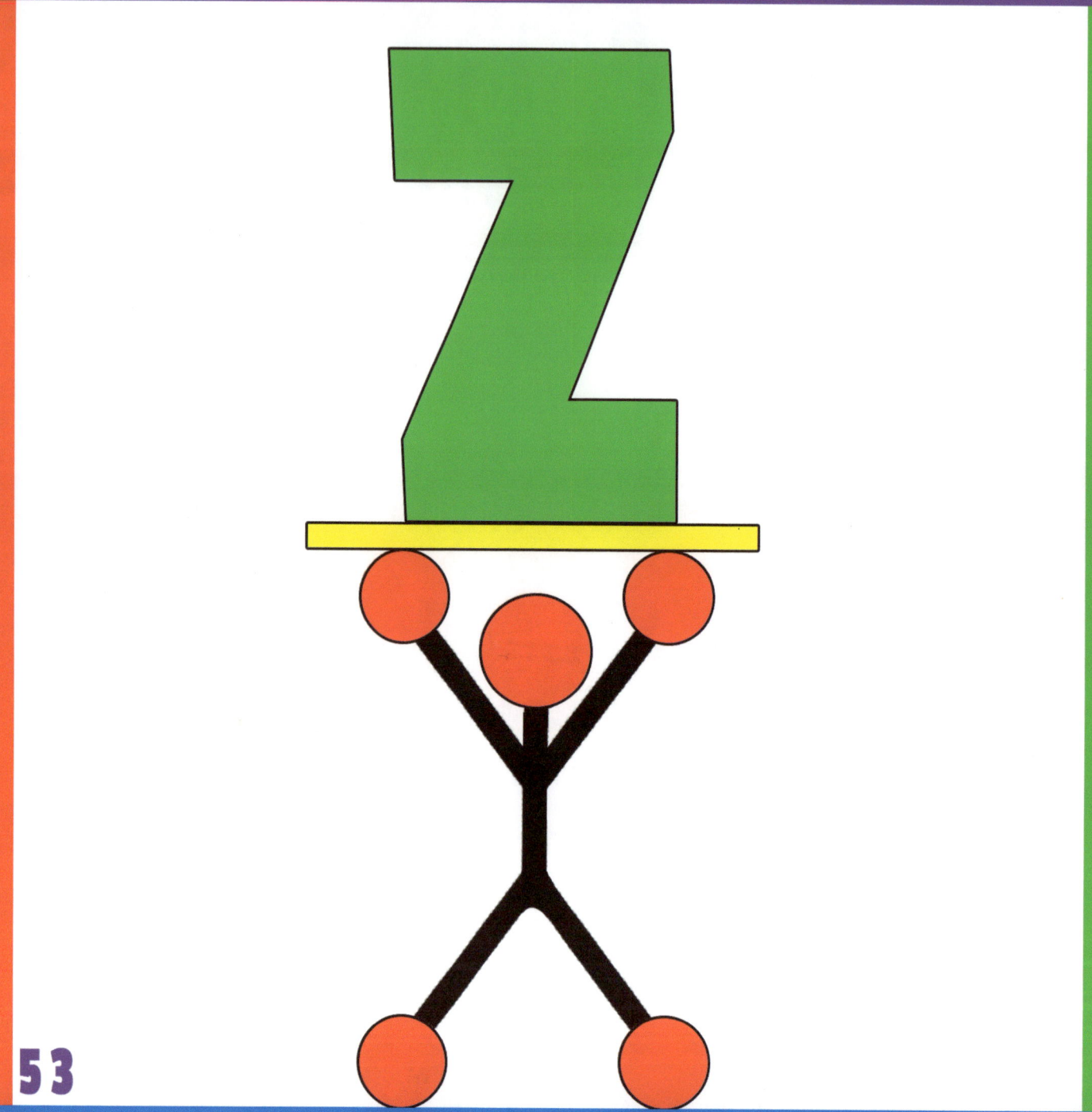

I zip for ZION!

PSALM 99:2

www.ingramcontent.com/pod-product-compliance
Lightning Source LLC
LaVergne TN
LVHW071026070426
835507LV00002B/39